Here's One I Wrote Earlier
Year 2

Here's One I Wrote Earlier

Instant resources for modelled and shared writing

Year 2

Gill Matthews and Gill Howell

Learning Matters

Acknowledgements

Page 32: B, Beautiful B!, ©Judith Nicholls 2002, reprinted by permission
            of the author.

Pages   Modelled on the book Owl Babies. Text © 1992 Martin Waddell.
41–49:   Illustrations © 1992 Patrick Benson. Used by permission of
            Walker Books Ltd, London.

Page 52: On the Ning Nang Nong by Spike Milligan from
            Silly Verse for Kids.

First published in 2002 by Learning Matters Ltd.

British Library Cataloguing in Publication Data
A CIP record for this book is available from the British Library.

ISBN 1 903300 51 7

Cover and text design by Topics – The Creative Partnership
Project management by Deer Park Productions
Typeset by Pentacor Book Design
Printed and bound in Great Britain by Ashford Colour Press

Learning Matters Ltd
58 Wonford Road
Exeter EX2 4LQ
Tel: 01392 215560
Email: info@learningmatters.co.uk
www.learningmatters.co.uk

Contents

Introduction

Here's One I Wrote Earlier, as the name suggests, offers you a substantial bank of examples of writing that you can use in modelled and shared writing sessions.

Demonstrating how to approach a particular piece of writing, or an aspect of the writing process, is an extremely effective teaching strategy. However, to think of ideas and to prepare resources for these sessions can be time consuming – and often challenging.

The examples provided here range from brief character sketches to stories to non-fiction reports. Fiction, poetry, plays and non-fiction examples are all included. The examples are at different stages of development – from a planning frame, to an outline draft and then to a polished version – so you can use them to take children through the whole writing process.

What are modelled and shared writing?

Modelled and shared writing take place during the whole-class session of the literacy hour. They are used to demonstrate specific skills and strategies used by writers. Modelled writing involves the teacher in creating the piece of writing in front of the class. Shared writing is collaborative – the children make suggestions for content, choice of vocabulary, sentence construction, etc.

Children often think that experienced writers write perfectly all the time. It is important, therefore, that when using both teaching strategies, you talk to the children about how you write, e.g. rehearsing sentences out loud before writing them down, explaining choices of particular words and phrases, discussing possible spelling options. It is useful sometimes to make mistakes – and to demonstrate how to edit and improve a piece of writing as you write.

To keep the children interested during modelled and shared writing, you could involve them by using interactive techniques, e.g. asking questions, giving quick individual writing tasks on the whiteboard, taking time out for discussions, asking the children to come out to the front to write. Make sure that all the children can see – and reach – the writing surface. When appropriate, write on paper rather than a wipe-clean surface as this will mean the writing can be returned to for further work.

How to use this book

There are two ways to find appropriate writing examples in this book:

- Page v lists the content of the book by literacy focus. Use this page to find, for example, samples of character profiles or instructions.
- The grid on page ix lists the NLS teaching objectives covered and the relevant examples of writing.

The examples are organised by term and in groups that take you through the development of a piece of writing. **All the examples in the book may be photocopied**. Some examples have been annotated so you can use them to focus on specific teaching points (for example, pages 8, 10, 18, 35, 37, 47, 48, 49 and 58).

Each page is organised in the same way to help you find your way around each example quickly and easily. Each example is prefaced by contextual information and is linked clearly to the NLS teaching objectives.

You'll also find suggested writing activities after each example:

 This indicates suggestions for teacher-led activities when working with the whole class.

 This indicates suggestions for activities the children could complete independently, either on their own, in pairs or in groups.

You may wish to remove the activities section at the bottom of the page and then enlarge the page, or make copies for use on an OHP. In some instances, you could give copies to the children for them to work on independently. Equally, you couod use them for ideas and present them as if you had written them earlier!

Stimulus material

Wherever possible, the topics chosen for writing for each term have been linked to provide continuity. The examples are based on the identified range of texts for reading and writing in the NLS *Framework for teaching*, and some non-fiction writing has links to other curricular areas. Traditional tales and rhymes are used frequently as these provide a well-known basis that allows children to focus on the writing process rather than be diverted by unfamiliar or challenging content.

Planning grid

To aid planning, this grid refers to word, sentence and text level teaching objectives in the NLS *Framework for teaching*.

Term 1

Word level	Page	Sentence level	Page	Text level	Page
		2	7, 9, 16	4	7, 8, 9, 10
		4	4, 16, 19	10	1, 2, 3, 4, 5, 6, 7, 8, 9, 10
		6	4, 16	11	7, 8, 9, 10
				12	11, 12, 13
				15	14, 15, 16, 17, 18, 19
				16	14, 15, 16, 17, 18, 19

Term 2

Word level	Page	Sentence level	Page	Text level	Page
		3	30, 31, 34, 35, 36	13	20, 21, 22, 23, 24
		6		14	25, 26, 27, 28, 29, 30, 31, 34, 35, 36, 37
				15	32, 33
				20	34, 35, 36, 37
				21	38, 39, 40

Term 3

Word level	Page	Sentence level	Page	Text level	Page
10	44, 47, 48	5	41, 42, 43, 44, 45, 55, 59	10	41, 42, 43, 44, 45, 46, 47, 48, 49
				11	50, 51, 52, 53
				12	54, 55
				19	60
				21	56, 57, 58, 59

**Term 1
Fiction**

Stories with familiar settings
Main focus Outline story plan using writing frame
NLS teaching objective T10

Chicken Licken

Beginning

An acorn fell onto Chicken Licken's head. She thought the sky was falling and ran to tell the King.

Middle

On the way she told her friends, Ducky Lucky and Goosey Loosey. They all ran to tell the King. Then they met Foxy Loxy. He said he would take them to the King.

End

Foxy Loxy took them to his den. Then he ate Chicken Licken and her friends. So the King never knew the sky was falling.

Activity

- Model how to write the beginning, middle and end of a known story.

Term 1 Fiction

Stories with familiar settings
Main focus Writing frame
NLS teaching objective T10

Beginning

Middle

End

 • Model how to plan a story using known story example.

 • Use to draft ideas for a story.

Term 1 Fiction

Stories with familiar settings
Main focus Model text
NLS teaching objective T10

Beginning

Some leaves fell on a kitten's head. She thought the tree was falling down, and ran to tell the farmer.

Middle

On the way she met her friends, the calf, the lamb and the duckling. They all ran to tell the farmer. Then they met the old sheepdog.

End

The sheepdog barked and growled at them, so they ran away. The farmer never knew that the tree was falling down.

Activities

 • Model how to base a new story on a known story.

 • Use as the basis for adding detail, orally, to a new story

Term 1 Fiction

Stories with familiar settings
Main focus Story staircase
NLS teaching objectives S4, S6, T10

Beginning

Ending

Activities

- Use as frame to plot story outline, showing simple stages of development.

- Draft story planner.

Term 1 Fiction

Stories with familiar settings
Main focus Story staircase – known story
NLS teaching objective T10

Beginning

Chicken Licken was walking through the woods when an acorn fell on her head.

Build up plot

She ran to tell the King and met her friends along the way.

Complication

They met a fox. He pretended to help, but led them to his den.

Ending

The fox ate Chicken Licken and her friends.

Activity

• Use as frame to plot story outline, showing simple stages of development.

Term 1 Fiction

Stories with familiar settings
Main focus Model text
NLS teaching objective T10

Beginning

Milly Mouse was walking through the fields when she trod in a puddle.

Build up plot

She ran to tell the farmer and met her friends along the way, Vera Vole and Ronnie Rat.

Complication

They met a giant cat called Cuddles. He pretended to help, but led them through his cat flap.

Ending

The farmer's wife saw the cat and rescued Milly and her friends.

Activity

- Use as model text, showing simple stages of development.

Term 1 Fiction

Stories with familiar settings
Main focus Model text
NLS teaching objectives S2, T4, T10, T11

Chicken Licken

One day, when Chicken Licken was walking in the wood, an acorn fell from a tall oak tree and hit her on the head.

'Oh no!' cried Chicken Licken. 'The sky must be falling down. I must run and tell the King.'

So Chicken Licken set off to find the King and tell him the bad news.

As she ran through the wood, she met Ducky Lucky. So Chicken Licken and Ducky Lucky both ran to tell the King.

After a while they saw Goosey Loosey.

'Oh! Goosey Loosey,' they cried. 'The sky is falling down. We must run and tell the King.'

So Goosey Loosey, Ducky Lucky and Chicken Licken all ran through the wood to find the King.

Next they met Foxy Loxy

'Where are you all going in such a hurry?' he asked, smiling his foxy smile.

'The sky is falling down,' they cried. 'We are going to find the King.'

'I know where he is.' said Foxy Loxy. 'Follow me.'

Then Foxy Loxy led Chicken Licken, Ducky Lucky and Goosey Loosey straight to his den.

After his huge supper of chicken, duck and goose stew, he sat outside his den and smiled his foxy smile.

And the King never knew that the sky was falling down.

Activities

- Use as a model to show how the language of time can structure the sequence of events.

- Identify and circle the time connectives.

7

Term 1 Fiction

Stories with familiar settings
Main focus Annotated model text
NLS teaching objectives T10, T11

Chicken Licken

Sets events at beginning of story

(One day, when) Chicken Licken was walking in the wood, an acorn fell from a tall oak tree and hit her on the head.

'Oh no!' cried Chicken Licken. 'The sky must be falling down. I must run and tell the King.'

(So then) Chicken Licken set off to find the King and tell him the bad news.

Cause and effect connective

As she ran through the wood, she met Ducky Lucky. So Chicken Licken and Ducky Lucky both ran to tell the King.

(After a while) they saw Goosey Loosey.

Passage of time

'Oh! Goosey Loosey,' they cried. 'The sky is falling down. We must run and tell the King.'

(So) Goosey Loosey, Ducky Lucky and Chicken Licken all ran through the wood to find the King.

Cause and effect

(Next) they met Foxy Loxy

Time connective

'Where are you all going in such a hurry?' he asked, smiling his foxy smile.

'The sky is falling down,' they cried. 'We are going to find the King.'

'I know where he is.' said Foxy Loxy. 'Follow me.'

Time connective

(Then) Foxy Loxy led Chicken Licken, Ducky Lucky and Goosey Loosey straight to his den.

After his huge supper of chicken, duck and goose stew, he sat outside his den and smiled his foxy smile.

And (in the end) the King never knew that the sky was falling down.

Clear final event

Activity

- Use as a model to show how the language of time can be used to show the sequence of events.

Term 1 Fiction

Stories with familiar settings
Main focus Model text
NLS teaching objectives S2, T4, T10, T11

Milly Mouse

One sunny day, when Milly Mouse was wandering through the fields, she suddenly stepped into a puddle, which went right up to her middle.

'Oh goodness,' she thought. 'The fields are flooding! I must run and tell the farmer.'

So off she set as fast as she could run. On the way through the field she met her friend, Vera Vole.

'Oh Vera Vole,' cried Milly, 'the fields are flooding. We must run and tell the farmer.'

Then Milly Mouse and Vera Vole ran to tell the farmer that the field was flooding. Soon they met their friend, Ronnie Rat.

'Oh Ronnie Rat,' they cried, 'the fields are flooding. We must run and tell the farmer.'

At once the three friends raced out of the field to the farmhouse, when suddenly they met Cuddles, the giant farmhouse cat.

'Where are you off to in such a hurry?' he asked.

'Oh Sir,' they replied, 'the fields are flooding and we are off to tell the farmer.'

Cuddles looked at the clear blue sky and smiled.

'I can help you find the farmer.' said Cuddles.

Then, as Cuddles led the three friends into the barn, the farmer's wife saw them. She grabbed a broom and chased them away.

So in the end, the farmer never knew his field was flooded.

Activities

- Use as a model based on a known story.

- Identify and circle the time connectives.

Term 1 Fiction

Stories with familiar settings
Main focus Annotated model text
NLS teaching objectives T4, T10, T11

Opening to set the scene

(One sunny day,) when Milly Mouse was wondering through the fields, she suddenly stepped into a puddle, which went right up to her middle.

'Oh goodness,' she thought. 'The fields are flooding! I must run and tell the farmer.'

So off she set as fast as she could run. On the way through the field she met her friend, Vera Vole.

'Oh Vera Vole,' cried Milly, 'the fields are flooding. We must run and tell the farmer.'

Time connectiv

(Then) Milly Mouse and Vera Vole ran to tell the farmer that the field was flooding. (Soon) they met their friend, Ronnie Rat.

'Oh Ronnie Rat,' they cried, 'the fields are flooding. We must run and tell the farmer.'

(At once,) the three friends raced out of the field to the farmhouse, when suddenly they met Cuddles, the giant farmhouse cat.

Shows time with a sense of urgency

'Where are you off to in such a hurry?' he asked.

'Oh Sir,' they replied, 'the fields are flooding and we are off to tell the farmer.'

Cuddles looked at the clear blue sky and smiled.

'I can help you find the farmer.' said Cuddles.

Then, as Cuddles led the three friends into the barn, the farmer's wife saw them. She grabbed a broom and chased them away.

(So in the end,) the farmer never knew his field was flooded.

Closing event

Activity

- Use as a model based on a known story to show how time words can show the structure of events.

Term 1 Fiction

Poems with familiar settings
Main focus Familiar poem as model for writing
NLS teaching objective T12

Incy Wincy Spider

Incy Wincy Spider
Climbed up the water spout
Down came the rain
And washed the spider out
Up came the sun
And dried up all the rain
So Incy Wincy Spider
Climbed up the spout again

Activity

 • Use as a model to demonstrate simple poetry structures.

Term 1 Fiction

Poems with familiar settings
Main focus New poem based on model of a familiar poem
NLS teaching objective T12

Incy Wincy Spider

Incy Wincy Spider
Climbed up the garden wall
Down came a brick
And made the spider fall
Up got the spider
Wincing with the pain
But brave little Incy
Climbed up the wall again

Activity

 • Use as a model to demonstrate substituting own ideas based on a familiar poem.

Term 1 Fiction

Poems with familiar settings
Main focus Writing frame
NLS teaching objective T12

Incy Wincy Spider

Incy Wincy Spider
Climbed up
Down came
And
Up
And
So

- Use as a frame to demonstrate innovating on a known poem's structure. Do not be concerned about rhyme, but model keeping rhythm.

- Use as a basis for writing own poem based on *Incy Wincy Spider*.

Term 1
Non-fiction

Instructions
Main focus Sequencing instructions
NLS teaching objective T15, T16

How to find the King

1. Go north out of the wood and into the field.

2. Go east across the field to the farm.

3. Take the road north from the farm, and go over the bridge.

4. Turn left into the meadow. Continue west to the far side.

5. Run past the fox's den. You will see the King's castle straight ahead.

6. Knock on the castle door and ask for the King.

Activities

 • Enlarge, cut out and model how to sequence numbered instructions.

 • Put the instructions into numbered order.

Term 1
Non-fiction

Instructions
Main focus Sequencing instructions
NLS teaching objectives T15, T16

How to find the King

Term 1
Non-fiction

Instructions
Main focus Writing frame – instructions
NLS teaching objectives S2, S4, S6, T15, T16

How to find the King

In the event that you notice the sky is falling down, you must inform the King by taking the following actions:

1. First go north...

2. Next go east...

3. Then take...

4. Turn left...

5. Run past...

6. Finally

Term 1
Non-fiction

Instructions
Main focus Model text
NLS teaching objectives T15, T16

How to find the King

In the event that you notice the sky is falling down, you must inform the King by following these instructions.

You will need a compass.

Step 1: Go north out of the wood. You will immediately see a field ahead of you.

Step 2: Turn right and go eastward through the field until you reach the farm.

Step 3: At the farm, warn the people as quickly as possible. Collect friends to help you on the journey if possible. Then take the north road until you come to a bridge. Cross over the bridge.

Step 4: Turn immediately left into the wide meadow.

Step 5: Avoid the fox's den in the meadow, and you will see the King's castle ahead in the distance.

Step 6: When you reach the castle, knock firmly on the door and ask to inform the King.

Activities

• Use as a model of how to write step by step directions.

Term 1
Non-fiction

Instructions
Main focus Annotated model text
NLS teaching objectives T15, T16

Title

How to find the King

In the event that you notice the sky is falling down, you must inform the King by following these instructions.

Explanation of purpose

You will need a compass.

What you need detailed first

Addresses the reader

Step 1: Go north out of the wood. You will immediately see a field ahead of you.

Clear numbered sequence

Step 2: Turn right and go eastward through the field until you reach the farm.

Step 3: At the farm, warn any occupants as quickly as possible. Collect companions to help you on the journey if possible. Then take the north road until you come to a bridge. Cross over the bridge.

Command at start of sentence

Step 4: Turn immediately left into the wide meadow.

Step 5: Avoid the fox's den in the meadow, and you will see the King's castle ahead in the distance.

Step 6: When you reach the castle, knock firmly on the door and ask to inform the King.

Time sequence words

Activity

 • Use as a model of how to write step by step directions.

Term 1
Non-fiction

Instructions
Main focus Improving instructions
NLS teaching objectives S4, T15, T16

How to find the king

In the event that you notice the sky is falling down, you must inform the King.

First of all, you should go out of the wood. When you see a field go across the field.

At the farm, you can tell the others. Then go on the road as far as a bridge.

Secondly you should go into the wide meadow.

Next in the meadow you should watch out for the fox's den in the meadow, and secondly you will see the King's castle ahead in the distance.

Go up to the castle. Knock on the door.

Thirdly and finally, tell the King.

Activities

- Discuss with the class why these instructions are unclear, and how they could be improved.

- Re-write the instructions so that they are clear, taking care to ensure a clear sequence of steps.

**Term 2
Fiction**

Settings
Main focus Planning frame
NLS teaching objectives S6, T13

Setting
Where?
Sights: what can you see?
Sounds: what can you hear?
Smell: what can you smell?
Touch: what can you feel?

Activities

 • Use to demonstrate making notes to describe a setting. Think about the senses of sight, smell, touch and hearing.

 • Make notes to describe settings.

Term 2 Fiction

Settings
Main focus Model text
NLS teaching objective T13

Setting
Where and when? The forest in the evening.
Sights: what can be seen? Trees, dappled sunlight on bark; rays of light through leaves from setting sun; long grass and thick undergrowth; foxgloves and other wild flowers; gloomy dark corners; branches hanging low; deep shadows full of menace.
Sounds: what can be heard? Rustling of leaves in the breeze; rustling of animals; sighing sound as wind blows through branches.
Smell: what can be smelled? Damp soil smells; crushed grass and moss.
Touch: what can be felt? Damp long grass brushing against legs; mossy path under feet; stinging of branches scratching face and arms.

Activity

 • Use as an example of notes on setting focusing on the senses.

**Term 2
Fiction**

Settings
Main focus Model text
NLS teaching objective T13

In the forest

As he went into the forest, the setting sun dappled the bark on the tree trunks, and the last rays of light filtered through the leaves. The long grass under the trees was filled with foxgloves and other wild flowers. He tried to keep to the path.

The leaves rustled in the breeze, or was it the rustling of animals in the thick damp undergrowth? He heard a sighing that could have been the wind in the branches. They hung low enough to make his face sting as they scratched when he pushed through into gloomy corners. The mossy path brought the smell of damp soil upward as he approached the shadowy corners. They seemed full of menace.

Term 2 Fiction

Settings
Main focus Model text
NLS teaching objective T13

Setting

Where and when?

Outside the Prince's castle during the ball.

Sights: what can be seen?

Lights from every window; flags flying from many turrets; bright, colourful ball gowns of ladies entering; twinkling jewels; carriages arriving and departing; horses tossing their heads.

Sounds: what can be heard?

Hum of people talking; orchestra tuning up; rustling of ball gowns; stamping of horses' hooves; jingling of harnesses.

Smell: what can be smelled?

Perfume; trampled moss.

Touch: what can be felt?

Shiny silk fabric against legs as Cinderella walked up the steps; chill evening air.

Activity

- Use as an example of notes on setting focusing on the senses.

23

Term 2 Fiction

Settings
Main focus Model text
NLS teaching objective T13

Prince Charming's castle

Cinderella climbed out of her carriage and gazed at the gleaming lights shining from every window of the castle. There were flags flying from the turrets, and the sound of an orchestra tuning up mingled with the rustling of ball gowns, the hum of conversation and the stamping of horses' hooves on the gravel. Harnesses jingled as the horses tossed their heads, as if they were impatient to be away.

As she walked towards the entrance, the perfume of many bejewelled ladies mixed with the scent of crushed moss upon the path. Taking courage from the feeling of her silk gown brushing against her legs, Cinderella walked up the steps to the castle door and left the chill evening air behind.

Activity

- Use to demonstrate how to turn rough notes from planning frame into connected prose.

Term 2 Fiction

Character portraits
Main focus Character planning frame
NLS teaching objective T14

Character's name _____

What does _____ look like?

What kind of person is _____?

How does _____ move?

How does _____ talk?

Term 2 Fiction

Character portraits
Main focus Completed character planning frame – Cinderella
NLS teaching objective T14

Character's name Cinderella

What does Cinderella **look like?**
pretty face
big brown eyes
dark hair
slim
small
ragged clothes
bare feet
dusty

What kind of person is Cinderella**?**
kind
friendly
helpful
lonely
sad
easily bullied

How does Cinderella **move?**
nimbly
small steps
glides as she has little feet

How does Cinderella **talk?**
gently
patiently
softly
clearly

Activity

 • Use to demonstrate how to make notes about a character.

Term 2 Fiction

Character portraits
Main focus Model text
NLS teaching objective T14

Character description – Cinderella

Cinderella had a pretty face. Her big brown eyes were framed by her dark hair. She was slim and small, dressed in ragged clothes and had dusty bare feet.

Although she was a kind, friendly and helpful girl, she was lonely and sad, as she was always bullied by her ugly sisters.

She moved nimbly about the kitchen in small steps on her little dusty feet, and seemed to glide over the floor.

Even when her sisters shouted at her, she replied gently and patiently to them in her soft, clear voice.

Activity

- Use to demonstrate how to change rough notes from planning frame into connected prose.

27

Term 2 Fiction

Character portraits
Main focus Completed character planning frame – Prince Charming
NLS teaching objective T14

Character's name Prince Charming

What does Prince Charming **look like?**
tall
handsome
dressed in the best clothes
fair hair
blue eyes

What kind of person is Prince Charming**?**
rich
charming
lonely
kind

How does Prince Charming **move?**
on his horse
in a carriage
strides
surrounded by servants
charmingly

How does Prince Charming **talk?**
charmingly
deep voice
posh accent

Activity

 • Use to demonstrate how to make notes about a character.

Term 2 Fiction

Character portraits
Main focus Model text
NLS teaching objective T14

Character description – Prince Charming

Prince Charming left his horse and carriage outside, and strode into the room surrounded by servants. Everyone noticed how tall and handsome he was. He was dressed in the best clothes, with fair hair and blue eyes. It was hard to believe a man so rich and charming was lonely!

Although his voice was deep and very posh, he sounded very kind when he asked to see the girl who fitted the shoe.

Activity

- Use to demonstrate how to change rough notes from planning frame into connected prose.

Term 2 Fiction

Character portraits
Main focus Model text
NLS teaching objectives S3, T14

Dear Sir

I would like to join your girl group 'The Princess Babes'.

I think I would fit in well with your band, as I am slim and very pretty. I have long dark hair and big brown eyes.

I would like to be on stage and I am sure the audience would like me, because I am kind and friendly to people.

I am also a good dancer. I have small feet and can glide about the stage. My voice is clear and I have practised singing in the kitchens where I live.

I would also be useful in other ways. I keep things very clean and tidy, so after performances, I could sweep up the stage and clear everything away. I have had lots of practice.

I look forward to your reply.

Yours faithfully

Cinderella

Activities

- Demonstrate how to use notes to create a character portrait.

- Use as a model for own writing. Write your own application to join a pop band.

Term 2 Fiction

Character portraits
Main focus Model text
NLS teaching objectives S3, T14

Dear Pop Hero

I am applying to take part in the competition to find a new Pop Hero.

I would be a good Pop Hero, as I am tall and handsome with fair hair and blue eyes. I can move well, and can stride about the stage in a very charming way.

My voice is deep, and I can sing even better than 'Posh' can! I don't want to enter just for the prize money, as I am already rich. I want to meet new people.

One advantage I have for the competition is that I already have my own servants, so your staff can look after the other competitors.

Please accept my application.

Yours charmingly

Prince

Activities

- Demonstrate how to use notes to create a character portrait.

- Use as a model for own writing. Write your own application to be a Pop Hero.

**Term 2
Fiction**

Poetry
Main focus Stimulus poem
NLS teaching objective T15

B, Beautiful B!

I'm a
busy, buzzing,
black and yellow bumble-bee.
Bzzz, bzzz, bzzz,
you can't catch me!

I'm a
Bobbing, bouncing,
Belly-dancing butterfly.
Bib, bab, bob,
watch me reach the sky!

I'm a
bossy, bungling,
bumpy-jumpy big brown bear.
Oomps-a-daisy, bumps-a-daisy,
chase me if you dare!

Judith Nicholls

Activities

- Focus on the rhythm, rhyme, alliteration and choice of vocabulary.
- Brainstorm ideas for a similar class poem using a different letter of the alphabet (see page 33) or further verses for B, Beautiful B!

- Children can draft individual poems, either using a different letter of the alphabet, or further verses for B, Beautiful B!

Term 2 Fiction

Poetry
Main focus Model text
NLS teaching objective T15

D, Delightful D!

I'm a
daring, dangerous,
fire-breathing dragon.
Huff, puff, huff,
you'll miss me when I'm gone!

I'm a
dancing, dashing,
Dalmation type of dog.
Woof, woof, woof,
take me for a jog!

Activity

 • Use to demonstrate how to write a poem based on *B, Beautiful B!*
(see page 32)

Term 2 Fiction

Character profiles Dictionary of fairy tale characters
Main focus Recording ideas
NLS teaching objectives S3, T14, T20

Wolf

In lots of stories. Bad character.

Cinderella

Good character. Badly treated by her family.

Prince Charming

Handsome. Met Cinderella at a ball.

Little Red Riding Hood

Good character. Wore red cloak with a hood.
Nearly eaten by a wolf.

Goldilocks

Ate Baby Bear's porridge, broke his chair, fell asleep in bed.

Chicken Licken

Silly character. Thought sky was falling on her head.

Activities

- Use to demonstrate how to record ideas about fairy tale characters. Discuss how the character profiles should give information about the character, e.g. their appearance, personality, behaviour.
- Work with the children on improving these character profiles.

- Plan character profiles of other story characters.

Term 2 Fiction

Character profiles Dictionary of fairy tale characters
Main focus Improving character profiles
NLS teaching objectives S3, T14, T20

Bold print

6 The **wolf** is in lots of fairy stories like Little Red Riding Hood and The Three Little Pigs. He is a bad character ~~who always~~ wants to eat people.

2 **Cinderella** had to work very hard. Her stepmother and the ugly sisters were horrible to her.

5 **Prince Charming** was very handsome. He married Cinderella.

4 **Little Red Riding Hood** took cakes to her grandma. Her grandma was eaten by the wolf.

3 **Goldilocks** ate Baby Bear's porridge. She broke his chair and fell asleep in Baby Bear's bed.

1 **Chicken Licken** was silly. She thought the sky was falling on her head and scared all the other animals.

Numbers showing alphabetical order

Telling the story, not about the character

Activities

- Use to demonstrate how to improve writing by focusing on structure, content and use of language.

- Edit own character profiles.

Term 2 Fiction

Character profiles Dictionary of fairy tale characters
Main focus Model text
NLS teaching objectives S3, T14, T20

Chicken Licken: silly chicken who thought the sky was falling on her head.

Cinderella: girl treated like a servant by her stepmother. Married a handsome prince and lived happily ever after.

Goldilocks: naughty blonde girl who ate Baby Bear's porridge.

Little Red Riding Hood: girl who wore a red cloak and was tricked by the wolf.

Prince Charming: handsome prince who married Cinderella and lived happily ever after.

Wolf: bad character who tried to trick Little Red Riding Hood and The Three Little Pigs.

Activities

- Use to demonstrate how to write concise character profiles.
- Discuss the style and layout of dictionary entries.
- Focus on the use of fairly brief language.

- Turn character profiles into dictionary entries and create a class dictionary of 'Our favourite story characters'.

Term 2 Fiction

Character profiles Dictionary of fairy tale characters
Main focus Model text
NLS teaching objectives T14, T20

'a' / 'the' omitted

Chicken Licken: silly chicken who thought the sky was falling on her head.

Cinderella: girl treated like a servant by her stepmother. Married a handsome prince and lived happily ever after.

Entries in alphabetical order

Goldilocks: naughty blonde girl who ate Baby Bear's porridge.

Little Red Riding Hood: girl who wore a red cloak and was tricked by the wolf.

Details about character

Prince Charming: handsome prince who married Cinderella and lived happily ever after.

Wolf: bad character who tried to trick Little Red Riding Hood and The Three Little Pigs.

Use of bold print for headword

Use of colon after headword

Details about character's actions

Term 2
Non-fiction

Explanation
Main focus Planning frame
NLS teaching objective T21

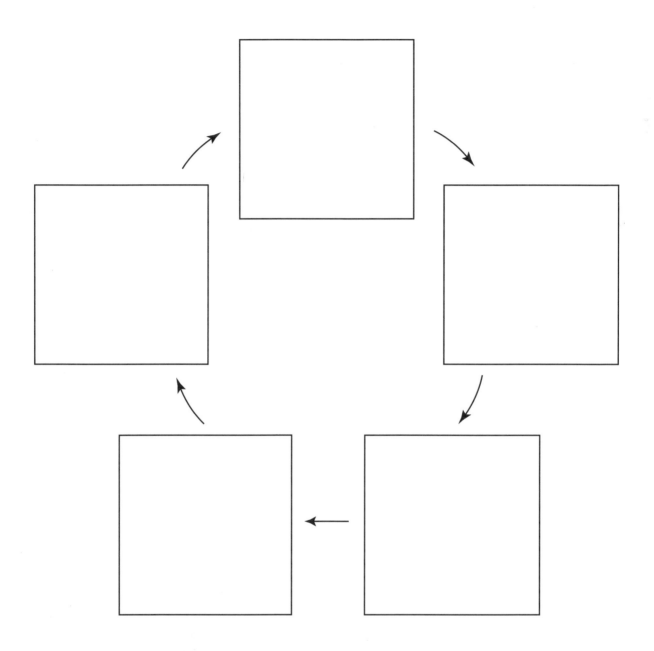

Activities

- Use the frame to demonstrate how to write and illustrate a simple cyclical process (see pages 39 and 40).

- Use the frame to write and illustrate a cyclical process.

38

Term 3 Fiction

Story opening
Main focus Model draft
NLS teaching objectives S5, T10

(This story opening is modelled on Owl Babies by Martin Waddell, published by Walker Books, 1992.)

Once there were three little puppies. They lived with a nice family in a nice house with a nice big garden. They liked their house.

One morning the three little puppies woke up. It was very quiet and they felt very cold. 'Where's our family?' they said.

The three little puppies had a good look round their house. They couldn't find anyone. 'Perhaps they've gone shopping,' they said.

**Term 3
Fiction**

Story middle
Main focus Model draft
NLS teaching objectives S5, T10

(This story opening is modelled on Owl Babies by Martin Waddell, published by Walker Books, 1992.)

But their family didn't come. The three little puppies got onto a chair by the window. They sat and waited. 'They'll come back soon,' they said.

They sat on the chair and looked out of the window.
They barked at the postman. They barked at the milkman.
'They'll bring us some nice dog biscuits,' they said.

They curled up together on the chair. 'I hope they haven't got lost,' they said. They closed their eyes and wished their family would come.

Activities

- Use to demonstrate how to base a story on an existing story.
- Discuss similarities and differences between characters, setting and plot in *Owl Babies* and this version.
- Focus on how a story middle involves a problem.

- Draft own story middles based on this draft and *Owl Babies*.

Story ending
Main focus Model draft
NLS teaching objectives S5, T10

(This story opening is modelled on Owl Babies by Martin Waddell, published by Walker Books, 1992.)

AND THEY CAME.

They drove up the road and parked outside the house.

'They're here!' they barked, and they bounced up and down on the chair.

'What's the matter?' the family asked. 'Did you think we'd got lost?' 'No!' barked the three little puppies jumping around and licking their family. 'We knew you'd come back.'

- Use to demonstrate how to base a story on an existing story.
- Discuss similarities and differences between characters, setting and plot in *Owl Babies* and this version.
- Focus on how a story ending ties up loose ends.

- Draft own story endings based on this draft and *Owl Babies*.

**Term 3
Fiction**

Story opening
Main focus Model text (see also page 41)
NLS teaching objectives W10, S5, T10

(This story opening is modelled on Owl Babies by Martin Waddell, published by Walker Books, 1992.)

Once there were three little puppies: Sally, Jess and Sam.
They lived with a kind family in a lovely house with a big garden.
They liked their family and they liked their house.

One morning the three little puppies woke up. It was very quiet and they felt very cold. 'Where's our family?' asked Sally.
'Oh my goodness!' said Jess.
'I want my family!' said Sam.

The three little puppies had a good look round their house.
They couldn't find anyone.
'Perhaps they've gone shopping,' said Sally.
'To get us food!' said Jess.
'I want my family,' said Sam.

Activities

- Use to demonstrate how to improve a draft version.
- Focus on adding dialogue and improving adjectives through the use of synonyms.

- Improve own draft story openings.

Term 3 Fiction

Story middle
Main focus Model text
NLS teaching objectives S5, T10

(This story middle is modelled on Owl Babies by Martin Waddell, published by Walker Books, 1992.)

But their family didn't come. The three little puppies clambered onto a chair by the window. They sat and waited.

A big cushion for Sally, a small cushion for Jess, and an old bit of rag for Sam.
'They'll come back soon,' said Sally.
'Back soon!' said Jess.
'I want my family!' said Sam.

They sat on the chair and looked out of the window.
They barked at the postman. They barked at the milkman.
'They'll bring us some nice dog biscuits,' said Sally.
'I suppose so!' said Jess.
'I want my family!' said Sam.

'I think we should all sit on my cushion,' said Sally.
And they curled up together on the chair.

'I hope they haven't got lost,' said Sally.
'Or had an accident,' said Jess.
'I want my family,' said Sam.
They closed their eyes and wished their family would come.

Activities

- Use to demonstrate how to improve a draft version.
- Focus on adding dialogue and improving language choices.

- Improve own draft story middles.

Term 3 Fiction

Story ending
Main focus Model text
NLS teaching objective T10

(This story ending is modelled on Owl Babies by Martin Waddell, published by Walker Books, 1992.)

AND THEY CAME.

They drove up the road and parked outside the house.

'They're here!' they barked, and they bounced up and down on the chair.

'What's all the fuss?' the family asked.
'Did you think we'd got lost?'
'No!' barked the three little puppies jumping around and licking their family.
'We knew you'd come back.' said Sally and Jess.
'We love our family!' said Sam.

Activities

- Use to demonstrate how to improve a draft version.
- Focus on layout of dialogue and improving language choices.

- Improve own draft story endings.

Term 3 Fiction

Story opening
Main focus Annotated model text (see also page 44)
NLS teaching objectives W10, T10

(This story opening is modelled on Owl Babies by Martin Waddell, published by Walker Books, 1992.)

Names given to characters

Once there were three little puppies: Sally, Jess and Sam.
They lived with a kind family in a lovely house with a big garden.
They liked their family and they liked their house.

Synonyms used to improve adjectives

One morning the three little puppies woke up. It was very quiet and they felt very cold. 'Where's our family?' asked Sally.
'Oh my goodness!' said Jess.
'I want my family!' said Sam.

Dialogue added

The three little puppies had a good look round their house.
They couldn't find anyone.
'Perhaps they've gone shopping,' said Sally.
'To get us food!' said Jess.
'I want my family,' said Sam.

Activities

- Use to demonstrate how to improve a draft version.
- Focus on adding dialogue and improving adjectives through the use of synonyms.

Term 3 Fiction

Story middle
Main focus Annotated model text (see also page 45)
NLS teaching objective W10, T10

(This story middle is modelled on Owl Babies by Martin Waddell, published by Walker Books, 1992.)

Improved verb

But their family didn't come. The three little puppies (clambered) onto a chair by the window. They sat and waited.

A big cushion for Sally, a small cushion for Jess, and an old bit of rag for Sam.
'They'll come back soon,' said Sally.
'Back soon!' said Jess.
('I want my family!') said Sam.

More detail added

They sat on the chair and looked out of the window.
They barked at the postman. They barked at the milkman.
'They'll bring us some nice dog biscuits,' said Sally.
'I suppose so!' said Jess.
('I want my family!') said Sam.

'I think we should all sit on my cushion,' said Sally.
And they curled up together on the chair.

Effective repeated dialogue

'I hope they haven't got lost,' said Sally.
'Or had an accident,' said Jess.
('I want my family,') said Sam.
They closed their eyes and wished their family would come.

Activities

- Use to demonstrate how to improve draft version.
- Focus on adding detail and dialogue. Also on improving verbs through the use of synonyms

Term 3 Fiction

Story ending
Main focus Annotated model text (see also page 43)
NLS teaching objective T10

(This story ending is modelled on Owl Babies by Martin Waddell, published by Walker Books, 1992.)

(AND THEY CAME.) —— Use of capital letters for impact

They drove up the road and parked outside the house.

'They're here!' they barked, and they bounced up and down on the chair.

'What's the matter?' the family asked. 'Did you think we'd got lost?'
'No!' barked the three little puppies jumping around and licking their family.
'We knew you'd come back,' said Sally and Jess.
'We love our family!' said Sam

Expanded dialogue

New line for new speaker

Activities

- Use to demonstrate how to improve a draft version.
- Focus on improving dialogue.

Term 3 Fiction

Poetry Limericks
Main focus Stimulus poem
NLS teaching objective T11

There was an old man of Fratton
Who went to church with his hat on.
'If I wake up,' he said
'With a hat on my head.
I know it hasn't been sat on.'

Anon

Activities

- Use this limerick as the stimulus for writing others (see page 51). Focus on the usually humorous content of limericks, the structure (5 lines), syllable pattern (usually 88668, although 9 and 5 syllables may also be used) and rhyme pattern (AABBA).

- Write own limericks.

Term 3 Fiction

Poetry Limericks
Main focus Model text
NLS teaching objective T11

There was a young boy in Year 2
Who didn't have much of a clue
He would act like a fool
When he got into school
In fact, he reminds me of you!

In Year 2 there was a young girl
Whose dad was a very rich earl
She was terribly bad
And it made him so mad
That his whiskers would quiver and curl.

Activities

 • Use to demonstrate how to write limericks.

 • Plan and write limericks using own names or those of friends.

Term 3 Fiction

Poetry Nonsense poem
Main focus Stimulus poem
NLS teaching objective T11

On the Ning Nang Nong

On the Ning Nang Nong
Where the Cows go Bong
And the Monkeys all say Boo!
There's a Nong Nang Ning
Where the trees go Ping!
And the tea pots Jibber Jabber Joo.
On the Nong Ning Nang
All the mice go Clang!
And you just can't catch 'em when they do!
So it's Ning Nang Nong!
Cows go Bong!
Nong Nang Ning!
Trees go Ping!
Nong Ning Nang!
The Mice go Clang!
What a noisy place to belong,
Is the Ning Nang Ning Nang Nong!

Spike Milligan

Activities

- Use as the stimulus for writing other nonsense poems.
- Focus on the invented words, rhyme and rhythm, and nonsensical content.

- Write own nonsense poems.

Term 3 Fiction

Poetry Nonsense poem
Main focus Model text
NLS teaching objective T11

On the Fing Fang Fong

On the Fing Fang Fong
Where the Sheep go Pong!
And the Tigers all say Poo!
There's a Fong Fang Fing
Where the grass goes Ding!
And the milk jugs Yibber Yabber Yoo.
On the Fong Fing Fang
All the rats go Twang!
And you just can't catch 'em when they do!
So it's Fing Fang Fong!
Sheep go Pong!
Fong Fang Fing!
Grass goes Ding!
Fong Fing Fang!
The Rats go Twang!
What a noisy place to belong,
Is the Fing Fang Fing Fang Fong!

Activities

- Use to demonstrate how to write a nonsense poem.

- Write further nonsense poems.

Term 3 Fiction

Book review
Main focus Model text
NLS teaching objective T12

Title: *Owl Babies*
Author: Martin Waddell
Illustrator: Patrick Benson

About the story:

Owl Babies is about three baby owls who think their mother has left them. They get quite frightened but keep telling each other that she will come back. It has a happy ending.

Best or worst things:

The illustrations are lovely. The baby owls look really cute and worried. I like the bit where the mother owl comes back and the baby owls are so pleased to see her. I would feel like that if I didn't know where my mum was.

Who will enjoy this book:

I think it is quite young children who would enjoy the book but they would have to have it read to them.

Activities

- Use as a model book review.
- Draw attention to the brief summary of the story and the justifications for the opinions expressed in the 'best or worst things' section.

- Write a review of a book read recently. The writing frame on page 55 could be used.

Term 3 Fiction

Book review
Main focus Writing frame
NLS teaching objectives S5, T12

Title:

Author:

Illustrator:

About the story:

Best or worst things:

Who will enjoy this book:

Term 3
Non-fiction

Non-chronological reports
Main focus Planning a report
NLS teaching objective T21

A report about frogs

Introduction
Amphibious – live on land and water

What they look like
Bulging eyes – can see in any direction
Webbed feet. Some have sticky pads on feet for clinging
Long back legs
Smooth or slimy skin – dull colour
Most 20–80 mm

Where they live
Anywhere in world – not Antarctica
Damp places

What they eat
Frog's tongue covered with sticky stuff to catch insects
Insects, worms, spiders
Don't chew – swallow food whole

Interesting facts
Over 400 species
Group of frogs called an army

Activities

 • Use to demonstrate how to plan a report.

 • Plan a report on a different animal.

Term 3
Non-fiction

Non-chronological reports
Main focus Model text
NLS teaching objective T21

A report about frogs

Frogs are amphibians. This means they can live in water and on land.

Frogs have a smooth, slimy skin. It is usually a dull colour. They have long back legs and webbed feet. Some frogs have sticky pads on their feet to help them cling onto things. Frogs have bulging eyes that can see in any direction. Their tongues are sticky to help them catch insects.

Frogs can be found all over the world except Antarctica. In the UK they usually live in damp, dark places.

Frogs eat small animals like insects, worms and spiders. They don't chew their food. They swallow it whole.

There are over 400 different types of frog. A group of frogs is called an army.

Activities

- Use to demonstrate how to turn a plan into a full non-chronological report.
- Focus on the use of paragraphs, the present tense and technical vocabulary.

- Turn plans into full non-chronological reports.

Term 3
Non-fiction

Non-chronological reports
Main focus Annotated model text
NLS teaching objective T21

Introduction
(includes definition)

A report about frogs

Frogs are amphibians. This means they can live in water and on land.

Present tense

Frogs have a smooth, slimy skin. It is usually a dull colour. They have long back legs and webbed feet. Some frogs have sticky pads on their feet to help them cling onto things. Frogs have bulging eyes that can see in any direction. Their tongues are sticky to help them catch insects.

Facts organised into paragraphs

Frogs can be found all over the world except Antarctica. In the UK they usually live in damp, dark places.

Frogs eat small animals like insects, worms and spiders. They don't chew their food. They swallow it whole.

There are over 400 different types of frog. A group of frogs is called an army.

Interesting facts

Term 3
Non-fiction

Non-chronological reports
Main focus Writing frame
NLS teaching objectives S5, T21

A report about

Introduction

What they look like

Where they live

What they eat

Interesting facts

Term 3
Non-fiction

Research skills
Main focus Recording information
NLS teaching objectives T19

What I know	What I would like to know	What I have learned

Activities

- Use the grid to demonstrate how to record existing knowledge about a topic, pose questions and record the answers after research.
- Discuss how to write in note form rather than full sentences.

- Use the grid during research.